A Portrait of Life Series (Portrait 4)

The
Pursuit of

Productivity –Economic success
Risk – Work – and more

J. Carl Jones
21st Century Philosopher

A Portrait of Life Series (Portrait 4)

The
Pursuit of

Money

Productivity –Economic success
Risk – Work – and more

ISBN-13: 978-1517192792
ISBN-10: 151719279X

Thank you Stephen Claypool—medical doctor, writer, entrepreneur, and philosopher. Your insight and technical assistance has been invaluable.

It has been said that philosophy is dead, and to a great degree it is. Pretty much all of the great philosophers lived hundreds or even thousands of years ago. They addressed questions of their time. Most of what they had to say has little relevance today.

To be meaningful in the 21st century, philosophy must speak to the people of our time. The writings of J. Carl Jones bring philosophy back to life.

XofLife1@gmail.com

Contents

Introduction

In a world of conflicting opinion there is a single point of agreement. We all agree that truth defines reality. At the same time, there is a second fact that breaks the harmony—everyone has a different opinion about truth.

Our view of the world is formed primarily by the culture we grow up in, along with our training and personal experience. For each of us this represents truth; and it can change, radically, from one individual to the next. We see our self and our culture as the center of the universe. We make this our point of reference.

Still actual truth is about reality. It requires that we examine real facts and draw appropriate conclusions—without bias or precondition.

The intent of this work (A portrait of life series) is to revisit our most basic concepts, to see how the facts really add up. Everything is referenced to observations that anyone can make. There is no hidden agenda, no special interest, just whatever the facts reveal.

Part I

_____#####_____

A story of economics

Chapter 1
(Productivity)

Modern economics began when one of our ancestors decided to stop foraging for food and grow it for himself. This was the beginning of productivity, a factory so to speak. Not only did it provide food, but it was also a form of employment. And with experience, productivity went up. He and his family could live better than ever before.

The farm/factory touches on two important points. First, it produces a necessity (food). And second, it produces in quantity. In modern America about 1% of the population grows the food for everyone; plus, we export. We feed the country, and the farmer makes a respectable living. Production of food is the first rung on the economic ladder.

With 1% of the population producing the food, the remanding 99% can do other things. The possibilities are endless. But how do we make it work? For society to prosper, the remaining 99%, or at least a reasonable portion, must engage in meaningful activity. Plus, the food supply must be available to everyone. We need a system that keeps everyone in the loop.

Other necessities

In addition to food we have other necessities, such as clothing, shelter, energy, and transportation. These are also produced in mass and engage additional people. Depending upon how we measure, about 5% of the population is directly involved in the production of necessities. In addition, for every person directly involved there is another person providing some form of support. Altogether, it takes about 10% of the population to provide for our basic needs.

Trade

At this point we have enough productivity to support a system of trade. Everyone involved can exchange goods to acquire whatever he or she might need. Of course, the barter system isn't particularly efficient. In which case, we add currency to make trading easier. A critical point in this plan is that consumption is linked to production. **One must produce something of value to acquire a means of trade—to consume we must first produce.**

The remaining 90%

Without the burden of producing necessities, the remaining 90% can do great things. They can explore the far side of the moon or map the human genome. At the personal level, they can provide services that improve the quality of life—even extend how long we live. But for these things to happen, they must be connected to the system of trade, or at least have access to its resources. *By in large, those who are outside the trading system find themselves among the world's underclass.*

Joining the system of trade

There is one simple requirement for becoming part of the system of trade—produce (or do) something of value. Then, when it's sold, we have the means to consume. We have joined the trading community.

Something of value

What do we mean by something of value? This is determined by the marketplace; if others are willing to buy it, it has value. The actual market value is determined by what others are willing to pay.

Two levels of connection

There are, in fact, two levels of joining the system. First is at the individual level, and second is as a community or society.

The individual level

At the individual level, joining the system can be as simple as getting a job. We sell our labor, which gives us an income; this, in turn, allows us to consume. We could also learn a trade or profession and then sell our skills. Another option is to start some type of business. At the same time, our ability to succeed is dependent upon the conditions we live in. An undeveloped society has little to

13

offer in the way of individual opportunity. A thriving community, in contrast, is a good place for the individual to advance.

The requirements

While producing (or doing) something of value sounds simple enough, in practice it's a major undertaking. Yes, it can be as simple as getting a job, but one must qualify for the job he or she is applying for. The typical entry-level job requires a high school diploma—that's 13 years of education. Becoming a professional requires even more training. Of course, there are lesser jobs, but they're limited in number and far less desirable.

As for the individual who starts a business, the majority of startups fail within the first year. Others survive but on the margins. For those who do make it, becoming well established can require years of dedicated effort.

The point is producing something of value is a serious undertaking. What's more, there must be a working system of trade to feed into.

The community level

On the collective side, every community must have some form of industry to support its economy. The industry will produce (or do) something which is sold to create an incoming flow of capital. This, in turn, supports jobs and trade. A functioning industrial base ties one's community to the larger system of trade.

Moving up

Sustainable industry

So, what does an undeveloped community (or country) do to improve its economic standing? There is a single requirement—acquire sustainable industry. Attract it; recruit it; build it—whatever it takes. And yes, it can be done. Hawaii is an isolated cluster of islands on the Pacific Ocean, yet it has a strong economy. Las Vegas was once a way station in the desert, but look at it now. Examples of joining the system go on and on. The primary requirements are imagination and perseverance.

Chapter 2
(Government)

The back door

There is a second option for tapping into the system of trade—the government connection. Instead of producing something of value, government uses the power of taxation to acquire funds. As mentioned earlier, productivity is the engine of economic success. Taxation, in contrast, uses resources without the requirement of producing. And without this restraint, there is a tendency for taxation to become excessive. At the same time, government does have important functions to perform. It also funds things that directly support productivity, such as research and the maintenance of infrastructure.

As to the direct affect of taxes, they are a drag upon productivity. As the tax burden increases the cost of production goes up. This, in turn, results in higher prices for the consumer and a general slowing of the economy. On the positive side, wherever tax money is spent there will be an increase in economic activity. However, this is not something for nothing.

The stimulus created will always be less than the tax required to support it.

Borrowing

At a second level, government has the ability to borrow and spend. And, again, wherever there is spending there will be an increase in economic activity. The appearance is that government is driving the economy. And it is—but only as long as the borrowing and spending continues. At the end of the day, any stimulus created will be temporary, and the debt must be repaid. Of course, there are times when borrowing and spending is appropriate, such as a national emergency, construction of infrastructure, or to create a short-term boost in the economy.

Finally

The bottom line is that taxes draw down the productive side of the economy. At modest levels, they have a limited impact. At high levels, they can be a major obstacle to the production of goods and services.

Chapter 3
(The wind down affect)

There is a fundamental problem built into the free economy—producers must compete to provide goods at the lowest possible price. Those who do poorly lose market share and may even be forced out of business. The result is intense pressure to hold down the cost of production—a primary element being the cost of labor.

The labor factor

Whenever wages are held down, spending by the wage earner will be limited. The result is a bottleneck in the economic cycle. Of course, when we consider a single employer, the affect is fairly minimal. However, pressure to hold down the cost of labor is pervasive. And over time, it slowly shuts down the economy—the wind down affect.

The solution is to keep wages up. The simplest way to accomplish this is for government to establish a progressive minimum wage. Of course, relying upon government can be an uncertain proposition.

Another approach is for employees to organize and negotiate as a group (form a union). Unions have proven to be successful at keeping wages up—which is the critical factor. At the same time, they have a well-earned reputation for corruption and predatory behavior.

In the end, the wind down affect is caused by pressure to hold down the cost of labor. Low wages then limit the money consumers have to spend, which slowly chokes off economic activity. For the economy to remain strong there must be a solid flow of money at every stage.

Chapter 4
(The great dilemma)

One day you travel to an undeveloped country. Poverty is everywhere; the quality of life is stark; children are begging in the street. You think to yourself, "I'd like to help, but how?" Your personal resources are far too limited to make a difference. You could contribute to a relief organization, but their ability is also limited. Even when wealthy nations become involved, success is minimal. Obviously, the people here would like to have a better life. They want the same things you want. So where is the problem? Why doesn't helping them work?

The problem
Clearly, such things as civil unrest, corruption, and crime stand in the way. However, beyond this, there is a single underlying requirement—there must be a working economy supported by some form of sustainable industry. This provides people with jobs along with an income to support their needs. When outsiders provide aid it helps, but when it is gone, things go back to the way they were. The underlying requirement is sustainable industry.

Industry

The historical pattern of industry is to locate in areas that favor operation. Individuals then follow the work. Some industries, such as mining, are location specific. Others, such as publishing, can locate almost anywhere and have contributors from around the world. With the advance of communications and transportation, more and more industries draw support from remote locations. More and more of the world is connecting with the system of trade—which benefits everyone.

Conclusion

It's becoming part of the larger trading system that allows a community to pull itself up. While there are numerous issues that can stand in the way, sustainable industry is the pivotal requirement.

Chapter 5
(Deceptive ideals)

The economic theories

The world has no shortage of economic theories—most with some degree of merit. The difficulty is long-term outcome. Every action called for by a theory triggers a chain of reactions. And there are so many possibilities that no one can accurately predict the outcome. The result is a collection of well meaning but uncertain concepts—deceptive ideals.

Performance
At the same time, we have been playing the game of economics for a long time. Almost any theory one could think of has already been tried. Although every situation is different, similar theories tend to have similar outcomes. In the end, past experience is our best indicator of future performance.

Capitalism or socialism
In this, the great clash of ideals is between capitalism and socialism, with each side touting its superiority. Interestingly, it's not the promise but the limiting factors of each that tells the real story.

Basic capitalism

It is generally agreed that capitalism, or the free market, excels in the production of goods and services. It's just not very people friendly. The rich get very rich and the poor get very poor. There is no concern for the environment or for human needs in general. Left on its own, it will cycle through periods of rapid growth followed by a crash, then economic stagnation. Eventually, market forces change and the process repeats. Still, beyond its problems, capitalism is the clear winner in terms of productivity.

Basic socialism

A primary goal of socialism is equality. This is accomplished through government control of production along with the fair and equitable distribution of goods. While socialism talks a good talk, its production side is a flat out failure. (It's not uncommon for a socialist society to have trouble feeding itself.) Distributing goods and services fairly is a great ideal—but only when there is something to distribute. The big question is why does socialism have such a great appeal?

The answer: It's intoxicating and deceptive. Everyone wants fairness. We see rich people with so much and others who are so poor. Why not spread the wealth around? What's more, when socialism is first tried it usually works. But over the longer term it slowly throttles back productivity. Eventually, there are shortages everywhere. The natural state of socialism is evenly distributed poverty.

Question: What is it about socialism that drags down productivity?

Answer: There is a fundamental conflict between EQUALITY and INCENTIVE. In a socialist society everyone's needs are taken care of equally—without regard to how well or poorly they perform. The process, by its nature, strips away incentive. And without incentive, productivity slowly winds down—creating socialism's great limitation.

Capitalism, on the other hand, rewards good performance and penalizes poor choices. It uses INEQUITY to move people to action.

Exceptions

There are, however, exceptions. Some countries finance social programs with outside income, such as the sale of natural resources. Because funding comes from outside the regular economy, the drag on productivity is offset. A small, oil-rich country can support numerous social programs and still maintain a high standard of living.

Think of it like a religious sect with oil wells. They may not be productive but they can live really well.

What works best?

To date, what has worked best is a capitalist system tied to a government that looks out for the people. The capitalist system is used to generate strong productivity. Government then sets minimum standards in areas such as environment, wages, and safety. Additionally, it supports social programs to ensure that basic human needs are met.

The challenge is to maintain balance. When the capitalist side becomes too strong its antisocial tendency starts to become a problem. When the balance tilts towards social needs, productivity begins to shut down. Clearly, the desired result is a tradeoff that maintains high productivity while, at the same time, supporting human needs.

As for the severe economic swings of capitalism, firewalls can be put in place. Key business sectors can be isolated from one another. Then when the stock market fails, for example, firewalls prevent the failure from spreading to other parts of the economy, such as banking. The problem is contained.

Overall, the capitalist system works surprisingly well, so long as government does its part—without overdoing it.

Automation

A common option for reducing the cost of production is automation. Machines are used to replace people. While this works for the producer, it's a job killer for employees. The result is displaced workers who must find other forms of employment. In a strong economy this can be fairly straightforward. However, when the economy is weak or there are a large number of layoffs, it can become a major problem. Still, when we consider the larger effect, automation improves productivity, reduces consumer prices, and frees people to do other things. Increased

26

productivity is the engine behind economic growth. Unfortunately, it often involves a period of transition.

Redistribution of wealth

When we consider the extremes of the poverty and wealth around the world, our first impression is that it doesn't seem fair. And the answer is clear—spread the resources around. There is no reason for anyone to want when the world has so much. However, there's a problem. Redistribution of wealth has been tried, in every possible combination, and it just doesn't work. There is a fundamental flaw built into this seemingly obvious solution. Spreading the wealth around puts all of the emphasis on one's need to consume while totally ignoring the concept of production. We have conveniently bypassed the first rule of economics—**to consume we must first produce.** For a solution to be successful it must begin with production. We then bring in consumption as a follow-up.

Protectionism

This is where a country taxes imports to protect existing business. One could easily support the idea that cheap imports will harm the economy. At the same time, an opposing theory insists that free trade will improve the economy. Clearly, both sides make good arguments. However, in actual practice, free trade consistently produces the best result.

27

The one-step solution

Finally, we come to the human side. People are attracted to one-step solutions. Again, take the idea of eliminating poverty through redistribution of wealth. It's so simple; it's almost poetic. So, where's the problem?

In the real world there is no such thing as a one-step solution. Every action sets off a chain of reactions. If we could stop the clock after equalizing wealth, the idea might have a chance. But the clock won't stop, and what follows is economic chaos. We must learn to think in steps greater than one.

Misinformation

As mentioned earlier, past experience is our best indicator of future performance. While this sounds simple enough, getting good information can be a major problem. In general, those who tell the story present it from their point of view. And this can include anything from an unintended skew to outright propaganda. It's hard to overemphasize the importance of working with good information. Economics is no different than any other field of inquiry; our conclusions can be no better than the information they are based upon.

All-in-all

The world has any number of economic theories—each with its dedicated supporters. But who can say what actually works? While the arguments aren't particularly useful, past experience is a fairly good indicator.

Part II

_____ ##### _____

Everyday life

While larger theories have their place, one's quality of life is defined, primarily, by everyday experience. This involves a series of smaller concepts.

Chapter 6
(Economic success)

Getting started

Young people, particularly, have almost no resources and aren't sure how to acquire them. Typically, the advice they're given is go to school, or get job. Of course, a minimum wage job pays barely enough to get by, and going to school can take years. The options aren't particularly attractive.

The big picture
This, of course, is how it's seen by someone who would like to connect with our system of economics. But the system they're joining is considerably larger and more complex than they imagine. It began before our country was even a country and has been slowly building and adjusting ever since. Within the system individuals acquire resources, or assets, and attempt to build upon them. Others will sell their labor to provide for their needs. Either way, coming up from the bottom is a major undertaking.

The multigenerational side
The classic case of getting ahead is multigenerational. In the late eighteen hundreds, a young couple moved west.

They settled on a small farm where they lived and were able to get by. Over the years they acquired a few cows, tools, and some additional land. Eventually, everything passed on to their children who further expanded the assets. Today, four generations later, they've grown into a progressive land and cattle company. Multigenerational accumulation is the most common way for people to acquire resources. It's a good system, if you come from a family with assets. As for everyone else, it's back to selling their labor to provide for their needs.

Jobs

Making a living

For most of the world, making a living is about getting a job, and not all jobs are equal. For someone starting out, this usually means taking whatever work is available and moving up from there. A starter job gets you into the system and moving. From here, most people will either advance with their current employer or—after a time—move on to another employer where opportunity is greater. After several steps, they'll usually settle into an acceptable position with reasonable pay. This is the most common option for connecting with the system. However, for those with a greater vision, there are other ways to go.

Adding skills

Clearly, anyone who is willing to learn a trade or acquire advanced training will have greater opportunity. Again, they'll need to start at the bottom and work their way up, but this time they're entering the workplace as a professional. In modern America the middle class is made up primarily of skilled and professional people. The key is to enter the workforce with meaningful training.

Meaningful skills

This is a problem area—not all training qualifies as meaningful. All too often students graduate from school only to find there are no jobs in their field. How do we avoid this problem? Simple; we check out a field before we begin training. *Talk to people who currently work in the area—they know the real story.* Can't find someone to talk to? That's a bad sign.

By the way, don't just accept a schools marketing pitch. This is one of the most important decisions of one's life. WE MUST DO OUR OWN DO-DILIGENCE.

Consistency of employment

Another concern is consistency of employment. While a specific career choice may look good, long stretches of unemployment (such as occur with seasonal work) can be a deal breaker. Meaningful employment is not just about getting a job; it's about staying employed.

Following the work

There are times when finding a job can be particularly difficult. (The economy is bad or a major employer has shut down.) The answer is to go where the work is. This, of course, means breaking with one's current support network and starting anew. It can be a tough choice. However, going without a livelihood can be even tougher. The solution is to follow the work and make a new life at the new location.

Employers

When considering a job, it's important to look at the employer as well as the work. While there are numerous things to evaluate, there are two telling points: turnover of employees and financial stability. When employees stay around for a long time, they must consider the job worth keeping. On the other hand, a large turnover usually indicates some kind of problem. As for the employer's financial stability, a tight budget will adversely affect both working conditions and payroll. An employer with means, in contrast, can afford to operate at a higher level. There are, of course, other considerations; but these two points establish a general frame of reference.

Self-sufficiency

The minimum requirement for personal self-sufficiency is ability to hold a job. Even an entry-level job will provide a regular income to support one's needs. Inability to stay employed, in contrast, leaves one dependent upon others for support. Self-sufficiency is about having a regular income, which essentially means staying employed.

34

Finally

It's finding a job that connects one to our system of economics. And it's finding a good job that allows us to live at a comfortable level. Employment is the gateway to self-sufficiency.

Making the money go around

Once we have an income, the next step is to make the money go around. In theory it's simple enough—we just don't spend more than we take in. In practice, however, there are a number of complicating factors.

Credit

Our first complication is credit—which allows us to buy now with the promise of paying later. It's a good system particularly for the purchase of larger items. At the same time, misuse of credit can be a financial disaster. We might compare it with fire—it's great for heating and cooking, but it can also burn down the forest.

Overspending

Having credit is an open invitation to overspend. There's a world full of things we'd like to have, and credit makes it easy to have them. Our promise to pay, in contrast, is an abstract. It is out there somewhere in the future. Given the imbalance between having things now and paying sometime in the future, there's a strong temptation to overspend.

Buying time

What credit really does is allow us to have things early. What we're doing is buying time, and it isn't cheap. The typical homebuyer will pay more in interest than for the home itself. Most car buyers pay as much in financing as for their car. Credit cards are also big business, and they have the highest interest of all. Credit, or should we say the interest on credit, erodes our purchasing power. Most people spend around one third of their income just to have things early.

Good debt

Not all debt is bad. Anything that pays for itself is good debt. A young man borrowed $150,000 to start a small construction business. Five years later the loan was paid and he owned everything outright. Because the loan enabled him to make money, we consider it to be good debt.

However, definitions can be tricky. Part of the money was used to purchase a truck. A basic truck would have worked just fine, but he bought one with all the frills. The difference between what was needed and what he purchased was luxury. In this case, part of the financing was good debt and part was bad debt—not that there's anything wrong with a little luxury. The point is we need to be aware of the difference and make our choices for the right reasons.

Finally

Credit must be used correctly. The rule is use credit when there is a clear advantage; beyond this, keep your distance.

Reoccurring expenses
The budget breaker

Any form of reoccurring expense is a parallel to credit, and the cost adds up just like interest. The problem is that we think in terms of a single payment—opposed to the long-term expenditure. Yes, we can afford $100.00 this month, but how about $3600.00 over the next three years? And how many of these expenditures do we have? Reoccurring expenses add up fast and can easily break the budget.

The human side

Making the money go around isn't just about balancing income against expenses. Right in the middle of it all is human nature—which is a child. It doesn't care about balancing the budget; it just wants what it wants. And there are lots of ways for it to disrupt our finances. In this, there are three particularly common problems: exaggeration of necessities, impulsive spending, and the more-is-better mindset.

Exaggerating necessities

Our first problem is that we're inclined to overstate necessities. It's a judgment call, subject to the whim of human thought. In practice, we add all sorts of things to our perceived needs. In fact, they can grow to the point of consuming the entire budget. For example, there is no question that food and shelter are essential. At the same time, a can of beans and a prime steak both qualify as food. Shelter could be a simple room or a trendy home. True necessities are the barebones minimum; anything more is exaggeration. We can't misrepresent our basic needs and expect to have control over spending.

Impulsive spending

In truth, everyone does some degree of impulsive spending. And it's harmless enough—so long as we're not spending money that should go to other things. The problem is when it becomes excessive. Add in a credit card, and things can really get out of control. Impulsive spending is the classic case of emotion overriding our better judgment.

The more-is-better mindset

For many of us, it doesn't matter how much we make. We adjust our lifestyle to slightly more than our income and then have trouble making ends meet. This is a mindset. We want everything we can possibly have and overreach to get there. If we'd just cut back on our lifestyle, balancing the budget would be a cinch.

Conclusion

Making the money go around isn't just about making enough to pay the bills. It's about managing things like credit, reoccurring expenses, and our own nature.

Chapter 7
(Resources)

While most of us live by selling our labor, resources can also provide a means of support. The difficulty with resources is they must be acquired and then managed—both are major undertakings.

Acquiring resources

Begin with a plan

The initial step in achieving almost anything—including economic success—is to have a plan. We need a step-by-step procedure to take us from where we're at to where we'd like to be. Without this our actions are without direction—which essentially takes us in circles.

At the same time, we must understand that no plan is perfect. It's important to make changes when change is required. Even our larger goals should be flexible. It's having a plan that keeps us progressing, and it's updating the plan that keeps us on track.

Getting started

The idea is simple enough. We just take part of our earnings and invest in something profitable. In time the investment will be large enough to produce a meaningful return. But, once again, we have the human factor. Most of us spend everything we earn; there is nothing left to invest.

The solution

A better choice is to live below our means, which leaves money to invest. Or, better yet, find a job that pays well, and live frugally. Consistency is also important; even a small amount invested regularly can produce a good result. The toughest part of acquiring resources is getting started. It begins ever so slowly and takes a long time to build. However, once we have momentum, it's comparatively easy to keep things going.

What to invest in

We all know people who have done well with their investments. The question is how can we copy their success?

Unfortunately, in most cases, we can't. Investment involves a changing landscape. Most success stories are about catching a trend, or opportunity, at the right time. It isn't just what we invest in; it's also about the timing. The requirement for us is to identify the opportunities of our time.

Where to look

Almost any time there is something new, or hot, or in transition there will be opportunity—which is our best option. Established fields also have possibilities. But they're fewer, and competition can be severe. Of course, it

40

is possible to just stumble into something, but relying upon luck is not a good strategy. In the end, most opportunity is driven by change.

Types of resources

Money

Let's face it; what everyone really wants is money—lots of it—enough money to live in whatever style he or she might choose. But in the real world, few people make this cut; it's the province of the very rich. And how does one become very rich? There is a single deciding factor—luck. In literally every case extreme wealth hinges upon chance—most often the chance of birth. Beyond this, there are a few people who win the lottery, find oil in their backyard, or become rock stars. And, finally, there are some who start at the bottom and make it all the way to the top. But, even here, it requires major breaks to rise to the level of extreme wealth.

On the other hand, acquiring enough money to live comfortably is within the reach of nearly everyone. At the same time, it does require planning, work, and perseverance.

Owning a business

A young man inherits a small hardware store. He makes himself manager and lives off of the profits. He is his own boss and earns more than he could by working for others. His income is essentially the profits of the business.

41

There are two important points in this example. First, the young man was not required to buy the business. Second, the business had a proven record of success—it was established.

Buying a business

It's also possible to buy an established business. Because it's currently running and successful, the risk of failure is low. It's finding money for the purchase that's a problem. In most cases, the buyer will make a small down payment and finance the remainder. While this is common practice, **too much debt can bankrupt an otherwise successful business.**

Starting a business

Another option is to start one's own business. It's less expensive than buying, but the risk is considerably higher. The majority of startups fail within the first year. On the positive side, one can start small and then grow.

Why the high failure rate

There can be any number of reasons for a new business to fail. However, there are two standouts. First is overestimating demand for one's product or service. (Be prepared for less traffic than even your lowest estimate.) Second is inexperience. (It's always good to have worked in a field or industry before starting out on your own.) Of course, there are many other potential issues, but overestimating demand and inexperience are at top of the list.

Income property

Another type of resource is income property—commonly rental houses or apartments. The main requirement here is having money to invest. Typically, the buyer will make a small down payment and finance the remainder. Rental income is then used to make the payments. It's a good system, but it does require ongoing management.

Is your home an investment

Think of it like this—we all need a place to live; we can either rent or buy. Rental payments never end. Home payments, in contrast, end when the loan is retired. Buying a home is investing in oneself.

Finally

When it comes to acquiring resources, the possibilities go on and on. The primary limitation is our own imagination. The point to remember is that once resources have been acquired they're capable of providing for our needs. They're worth working hard to get and just as hard to keep.

Summary

Personal economics aren't particularly difficult. The primary requirement is to do the basics, like learn a skill and stay employed. Aside from lucky breaks, getting ahead is mostly about working one's way up the ladder.

At a second level, having resources can also provide a means of support. The difficulty here is that resources must be acquired and managed—which is a major undertaking.

Chapter 8
(The stock market)

As the market falls and then drops again, everyone is concerned about the larger economy. And there are opinions everywhere. The question is does anyone know what they're talking about? It's time for a rational discussion.

The business side

At its core, selling stock is an innovative way for business to raise money (opposed to borrowing from the bank). Let's say a corporation needs to build a new plant. One way to finance the project is through the sale of corporate stock. (Each stock represents ownership of a very small portion of the company. If the company does well the value of its stock should increase resulting in a profit for investors.) The sale of stock provides money for the new plant without having to borrow. And investors, hopefully, will make a profit. It's quite an idea, almost as good as printing your own money. The whole thing has been so successful that corporations everywhere are doing it.

The market

The next step is for someone to set up an exchange where investors can buy and sell stock. The intriguing part about this is that stocks are just pieces of paper. Although companies like to keep the value of their stock up (They may want to sell more sometime.) it has little to do with the day-to-day operation of their business. In fact, there is no direct connection. The stock exchange is about trading; it's the trader who stands to lose or gain. It's like Las Vegas; you buy stock and play the game. Then, at some point, you sell the stock and take your profit (or loss). There is no specific linkage between trading on the stock exchange and the world of real commerce. A company's stock can drop to $1.00 per share and business will continue as always. On the other hand, stock can go to $100.00 per share and the company will still keep doing what it does. Again, there is no specific linkage between the stock market and the day-to-day operation of a company.

The exception

Question: Why then did the stock market crash of 1929 set off the Great Depression?

Answer: The stock market was sizzling hot before the crash. Everyone was making money. Even banks got into the act—trading with depositors' money. Then, when the market crashed everyone lost—including the banks. This set off a wave of bank failures. And without a viable banking system, the larger economy began to fail.

In the aftermath Congress passed the Glass-Steagall Act, which established strong controls over banking. (Note: Under pressure from the banking industry, Glass-Steagall has since been repealed.) The FDIC was also established—to insure individual bank accounts. Unfortunately, this all came after the fact. What we had was a failure of the banking system—triggered by the market crash.

The value of stock

Of course, every stock is backed by the value of its issuing company. As a company's fortunes rise and fall the value of its stock will track accordingly. *However, this works one way only.* What traders do on the stock exchange has little effect on business. So long as the stock market is isolated, other parts of the economy are not affected. The only way for the stock market to affect business is for business to start playing the market—or be entwined with someone who is.

A final question: Why even bother with the stock market?

Answer: The idea of selling stock to raise money only works when there is a way to buy and sell stock. The stock exchange provides a marketplace for both buyers and sellers. (It performs a useful service.) Our challenge

47

is to keep it—along with its erratic behavior—away from the general economy.

Trends in the market

When the market goes up, the trend could continue for as long as eight or ten years. Then, when it goes down, it could be there for another eight or ten years. During the up cycle, nearly everyone makes money. During the down cycle, it's difficult to get ahead, no matter what we invest in. It's important to understand the rhythm of trends and invest accordingly.

Follow—don't lead

Trends have two unique characteristics. First, once they begin, they can to go on, and on, and on. Second, predicting when they'll change is next to impossible— there are just too many variables. Given these characteristics, our best strategy is to wait for a trend to occur and then follow its lead. **At the same time, have a plan to exit on short notice.**

While this appears to be straightforward, there's a problem. It's just human to predict what's coming next. It's also human to invest according to our predictions. At the same time, until a trend actually begins, it's far from certain. Even when change is in the air, it's smart to let it happen before we jump in.

A time to get out

Eventually, every enterprise comes to the point of decline. By following the trends, we'll see it coming and make a timely exit. Just as there is a time to get in, there is a time to get out.

As for the sharp falls, it's important to know where to put in stops.

Chapter 9
(Risk)

At its best, risk can bring fame and fortune. At its worst, it can be ruinous. For the average person it's something to avoid. At the same time, risk is a force that can be channeled to our advantage.

Avoiding risk

A young man is smart, talented, and good looking; but he's afraid of risk. There's a lady he'd like to ask out, but he'll not—for fear of rejection. A business opportunity has come his way, but he'd never accept because it could fail. And so, he goes through life avoiding risk and never moving forward.

The risk taker

Another man thrives on risk. Although he has experienced numerous failures, he thinks of them as setbacks and keeps on going. One day he put everything he owned into a business venture. It came through beautifully, and he made a lot of money. Later, another opportunity came his way. Except, this time it failed, and he lost everything. He found himself back where he started twenty years earlier.

The window of risk

Putting everything on the line for a large gain can bring us up rapidly. But when we keep doing it, we're virtually assured of failure. It's like calling a coin toss. The first time we have a 50/50 chance of being right. Twice in a row, the odds drop to 25%. Three times in a row, we're down to 12.5% and so on. When we risk everything, over and over, eventually the odds will catch up with us. It's important to keep our window of exposure as small as possible.

Be prepared to fail

In every risk there is a chance of failure, even when the odds are strongly in our favor. The rule is we can't advance without taking some kind of chance. But when we do, we're exposed to the possibility of failure. Everyone loves winning. But what happens when we do our best and fail? Are we tough enough to pick up the pieces and go on? Or do we allow it to drag us down? This is where the real drama of life unfolds.

The elements of risk

There is power in risk. But to use it, we must understand the process. Actually, there are five interrelated factors: potential for gain, potential for loss, the odds of success, need, and human nature. Of these, need and human nature relate to the individual involved. Potential for gain or loss and the odds of success focus on the risk itself.

Potential for gain

The primary reason for taking a risk is to achieve some type of gain. This doesn't require much discussion except that it shouldn't be our only consideration. It's possible to become so focused on a potential gain that we overlook other important considerations. High-risk sports would be a good example. While a put-it-all-on-the-line mindset is good for achievement, it comes with a serious down side—one could be injured, or even killed.

Potential for loss

In every risk there is a potential for loss. It's important that we know, precisely, what it is we have to lose—right up front. Once we're clear on this, we're ready to consider other factors, such as need and the odds of success. That's the theory.

However, in practice, potential for loss is usually dealt with at an emotional level. Each of us has an internal setting for acceptance of risk. When the setting is exceeded, our thoughts lock into the problem and fear engages. As a defense system this works fairly well. However, if one's internal setting is too high, or low, or if there are outside considerations, things can go seriously wrong.

At the same time, we can manipulate our sense of risk. A soldier goes into battle knowing that he may die. In this case, a common strategy is acceptance: "I don't expect to make it back alive." Another strategy is to invoke fate: "When my time comes, it comes." At a lesser level, we've all been in situations where it's best not to look down. All in all, our first response to potential for loss is emotional. We then modify this with logical direction.

The odds

The odds of something happening is also a determining factor. There is a remote chance of being killed by a falling meteor. The cost (being killed) is severe. At the same time, the chance of it happening is exceedingly small. In this case, we ignore the risk and get on with our lives. We overlook any number of everyday risks because the odds are exceedingly small. Actually, we don't usually calculate the risk; we just do what every-one else is doing—which may or may not be smart.

A word of caution: Anytime you're asked to sign a release before engaging in some activity, know that it's time to recalculate the odds.

Need

Another factor is need. Why risk anything for some-thing we don't need? On the other hand, extreme need will cause us to take extraordinary risk. When the level of need is sufficient it will override nearly every other consideration.

Automatic response

In addition to other factors, we all have automatic responses. When a threat is sensed, it triggers a specific reaction—which could be anything from heightened awareness to outright panic. While our senses are good at flagging problems, the reaction is often a poor fit.

In contrast, any time we experience risk without apprehension, we have a problem. A classic example is the handyman who feels comfortable on a ladder—and then has an accident.

Summary

In general, risk taking is about balancing the potential for gain against the cost of losing. This, in turn, is weighed against the odds of success and our degree of need. Finally, we have emotions—which have their own mind and are capable of overriding every other consideration. Put everything together in one package and we have the essentials of risk.

The rush

When our senses pick up on risk, it creates an emotional rush. This allows us to respond with appropriate intensity—the greater the risk the greater the rush. It's exciting and makes us feel alive. In addition, it helps offset the fear of taking risk.

At another level, sports and recreational activities often simulate some type of risk. The effect is to make them exhilarating, which keeps us coming back.

Finally, beware, the rush can be addictive. Don't allow the chemistry of it all to take us to places we shouldn't go.

The ethics of risk

Endangering others

Up to this point we have been discussing personal risk. We make a choice; and if there's a cost, it's ours to pay. At the same time, the choices we make often affect other people, which is an entirely different matter. Drinking and driving is a choice that puts others in danger. At first glance, we think that no one has the right to endanger others. But risk is complex. For example, taking one's family on vacation will expose them to risk, yet we consider this to be acceptable. In both cases, we're looking at the danger of travel. The critical difference is the odds. Drinking and driving wouldn't be a problem if the odds of having an accident didn't go up. The point is, with so many factors, it's difficult to apply broad principles. In general, each situation must be considered individually.

Work

At an entirely different level, we have risk associated with work. Police and firefighters are routinely exposed to danger. The same is true for construction workers and miners. In this situation, the worker accepts risk as part of the job. The employer is then responsible for making the job as safe as possible. Again, we have a situation where one party's choices affect the safety of another. And, once again, there is the question of where we draw the lines.

In this case, there are two considerations. First, how great is the need? And, second, have we done everything possible to ensure safety? Clearly, we should never put someone in danger needlessly. And when we do accept risk, we should move the odds as far as possible in our favor.

Conclusion

Risk is a fundamental part of human experience, and it's often difficult to pin down. Generally, we just take it as it comes. However, by understanding the process and making good choices, we can tilt the scale in our favor.

Chapter 10
(Work)

The magic of work

If there were a magical cure for the world's ills it would be work. Work gets us up in the morning, requires us to go out and interact with others, stimulates the mind, and exercises the body. It takes us to new places and opens the door to new experience. It pays our bills and supports our way of life. It keeps our mind busy and gives us purpose. In addition, it produces the goods and services necessary for society to function. Work is one of the most positive forces of human experience—it's almost magical.

Note: This chapter is intentionally one paragraph long. Our point is to imprint a single idea into the reader's mind.

Chapter 11
(Doing what we dislike)

One of life's early lessons is that we must do things we don't like. At the same time, our instinct tells us to resist. The problem is that almost anything we want—or would like to achieve—requires something of us that we'd rather not do. And occasionally, it can be extreme. The answer is to accept this as a basic condition of life. And when the time comes, suck-it-up and do what's necessary. The alternative is to resist—which puts an end to whatever it is that we're trying to accomplish. By and large, individuals who practice resistance become the dropouts of society. The only way to achieve a goal is to do what's required—including the parts we dislike.

Management

At the same time, the unpleasant parts of life are not beyond management. For example: While it may be necessary to work for a living, there is no requirement to work at something we dislike. Quiet music, while doing something boring, can lift one's mood. Mowing grass during the cool of the morning is better than sweating it out during the heat of the day. Breaking a task into small parts will generally make it easier. Having the right tools or accessories is always a good idea. The point is that we're not just stuck with the least attractive option. In fact, in many cases we can actually turn an unpleasant task into something enjoyable.

A second point

For anyone who manages the work of others, it's important to create a positive work environment. Not only will workers feel better, but the quality of their work will improve.

Conclusion

The requirement of doing things we dislike is just part of life. Our best adjustment is to suck-it-up and get it done. At the same time, we do have the option of making things more agreeable. A key element of succeeding—at anything—is taking control of whatever is unpleasant.

Index

INDEX

INDEX

INDEX

A Portrait of Life (series)
by J. Carl Jones

Portrait 1—A Portrait of God
Humankind's most elusive quest—*God*—

Portrait 2—The Fringe of Understanding
Questions that exist on the fringe of understanding
—*Awareness – Meaning – Life - Death - Pain – Evil*—

Portrait 3 —The Deciding Factors of Civilization
— Ethics - Violence - The art of working together - Systems we use –and more—

Portrait 4—The Pursuit of Money
—Productivity – Economic success - Risk - Work – and more—

Book 5— A Portrait of Life
The full series in one book
—Life - Death - Pain - Evil - Awareness - Meaning - God - and much more—

All books available in large print

The Essential Human Values

Respect **Others**

Take **the High Road**

Be **of Peace as you walk through life.**